THE HOW AND WHY WONDER BOOK OF
DOGS

Written by
IRVING ROBBIN

Illustrated by
WILLIAM BARSS

Editorial Production:
DONALD D. WOLF

Edited under the supervision of
Dr. Paul E. Blackwood,
Washington, D. C.
Text and illustrations approved by
Oakes A. White, Brooklyn Children's Museum, Brooklyn, New York

PRICE STERN SLOAN
Los Angeles

Introduction

It would be amusing to visualize a curious dog nuzzling through the pages of this book to find a picture of itself, or perhaps a paragraph describing its particular qualities. Of course, dogs cannot read about themselves, but we are able to imagine such a picture because dogs are noted for their high degree of intelligence.

Through the centuries, dogs have been developed, or bred, for special skills — skills that man has used to his great advantage. Even though dogs now differ from one another according to breed, all of them developed from one grand ancestor, and dogs were already on earth at the time of man's first recorded history.

The How and Why Wonder Book of Dogs is generously illustrated with pictures and filled with descriptions of most present-day dogs. The book catches the spirit of the matchless usefulness of these devoted and versatile animals. It is a book for all young people to use at home or in school as they search for new and interesting information about man's best friend.

Paul E. Blackwood

Dr. Blackwood is a professional employee in the U. S. Office of Education. This book was edited by him in his private capacity and no official support or endorsement by the Office of Education is intended or should be inferred.

Contents

Older Than Man

Watch a child playing with a puppy, or a man out for a walk with his dog beside him. Notice how a blind man depends on his seeing-eye dog, or how a sheep rancher depends on his team of collies. Follow a hunter and see how his bird dog finds and flushes the game. These are common sights in the twentieth century — so common that we hardly notice them — yet each person is carrying on a tradition and a partnership as old as the human race itself.

To make an intimate companion of an animal is quite unique for man. Of all the animals that have served and still serve man in his long history, only the dog has become a partner, a companion and a playmate. What is also unique is the fact that this relationship has not been enforced. Both man and dog have come to it with a sincere affection and loyalty for each other. It is a tribute to both species that they can

MIACIS

Miacis, the grand ancestor of all dogs, preyed on the plant-eaters of its time.

The ancestors of today's dogs lived with man during the Stone Age.

live together not only in mutual dependence but also as friends. This is a special mark of distinction, for the dog family lived on earth many millions of years before man arrived.

The dog family has a history that goes back some 40 million years to the Eocene period, one of a long series of geologic eras in the development of the earth. Tiny horses, miniature camels and primitive monkeys inhabited the land during this period. They were herbivorous animals —plant-eaters—and completely peaceful. Preying on these animals was a small but ferocious carnivore—meat-

What is the history of the dog?

eater — that was adapted to both tree-climbing and running in the open. It was a long-tailed, short-legged beast and it made life miserable for the grazing animals. This tough little creature — named *Miacis* by scientists — was the grand ancestor of all the dogs, tame and wild, that we know today.

When the course of time moved our world some five million years from the Eocene to the Oligocene period, *Miacis* had sired a

What other animals are the ancestors of today's dogs?

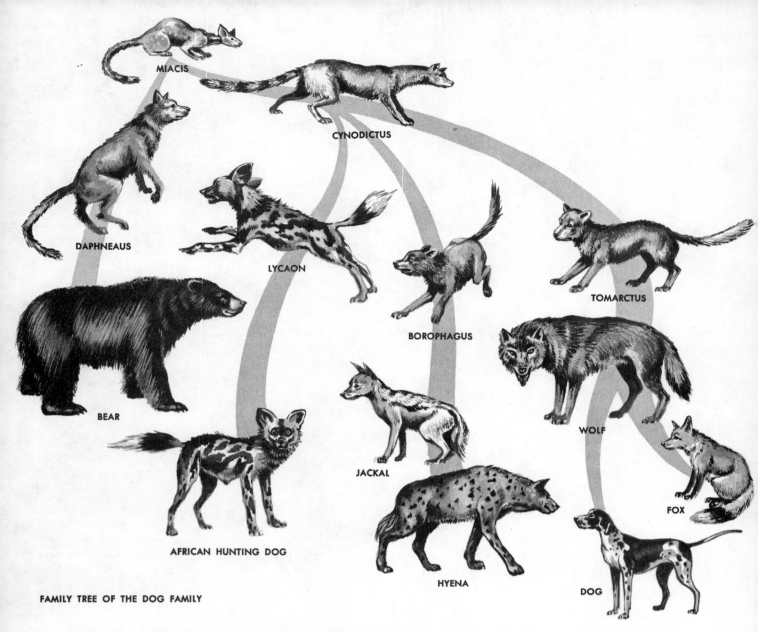

FAMILY TREE OF THE DOG FAMILY

family. There were two descendants. One was a heavy, ruggedly-built animal named *Daphneaus*, known as a "bear-dog." As millions of years passed, *Daphneaus* evolved into a true bear and was the father of our present-day family of bears. The other descendant was slim and lithe and is known to us as *Cynodictus*. It could no longer climb trees, its legs were longer and it had become a swift runner.

In the Miocene period, there were three descendants of *Cynodictus,* all of which looked very much like modern dogs. One, *Lycaon,* sired the wild breed of African hunting dogs; the other, *Borophagus,* fathered the jackels and hyenas; and the third, *Tomarctus,* stood at the head of the modern family of wolves, foxes and dogs.

What did Tomarctus look like? *Tomarctus* was quite wolflike in appearance, with its long bushy tail, small pointed ears and a runner's legs. In addition, it was fully adapted to chasing game. *Tomarctus* could run a deer hour after hour, never tiring. Its keen sense of smell allowed it to track quarry in the dark and tangled underbrush, and its sharply pointed fangs were designed for tearing.

Tomarctus had come a long way from the primitive *Miacis*. It was a true dog in almost every way. Yet the thing to remember at this point is that the dog and bear have a common ancestor. One must go a long way back in time to find the relationship, although both modern animals carry certain resemblances. But *Miacis* stands at the head of the line, a true founding father of the modern dog.

The meeting between man and dog

When did man and the dog first meet?

must have taken place at almost the same time that man became an intelligent, tool-using being. That was some 500,000 years ago. Fossils found in some of man's early cave dwellings indicate the presence of dogs. Actually the dog was man's first domestic animal. This relationship soon became a partnership, and early cave paintings show dogs helping men to trap wild game. It is conceivable that in those primitive times dogs also stood guard at their masters' caves, played with the young children and helped to haul loads.

One does not know exactly how man

How did man first domesticate the dog?

first domesticated the dog, but the most important clue to the answer lies in the nature of the dog itself. All dogs, even the wild breeds, are basically friendly, social animals that have the

BABYLONIAN DOG

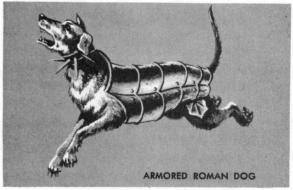

EGYPTIAN DOG

CHINESE DOG

ARMORED ROMAN DOG

From old paintings and reliefs, we know that the Babylonians used dogs for hunting, as did the Egyptians and Chinese. Ancient records also tell us that the Babylonians bred dogs as companions for ladies. The Romans used dogs to fight slaves and wild animals.

SPORTING DOGS

COCKER SPANIEL

AMERICAN WATER SPANIEL

SPRINGER SPANIEL

SPANIELS

IRISH WATER SPANIEL

FIELD SPANIEL

CLUMBER SPANIEL

BRITTANY SPANIEL

POINTERS

WEIMARANER

GERMAN SHORT-HAIRED POINTER

WIRE-HAIRED POINTING GRIFFON

SETTERS

IRISH SETTER

ENGLISH SETTER

GORDON SETTER

RETRIEVERS

CURLY-COATED RETRIEVER

LABRADOR RETRIEVER

GOLDEN RETRIEVER

CHESAPEAKE BAY RETRIEVER

ability to develop a strong attachment to human beings. There are outstanding examples of this fact. The Alaskan Malemute, a powerful sled dog, is wolf-bred. The Alaskan Indians raised wolf cubs until they became friendly and loyal animals. This same thing may have taken place in the dawn of human history.

Perhaps a litter of wild puppies was taken back to a cave dwelling and raised in the presence of people. Maybe a wild dog discovered that sharing the company of men resulted in protection, including easier access to food. It is a tribute to the intelligence and adaptability of the dog that it was able to take advantage of the relationship. The partnership proved to be fruitful.

The struggling human race, learning to live in a savage environment, found in the dog a loyal protector and devoted companion. Hunting became easier, the sounds of the night were less fearful — all because of the presence of a wild animal that chose to live with men.

No one is certain when the specialized breeding of dogs began, because recorded history began rather late. However, there are records of specialized dogs that go back 5,000 years. Some breeds, such as the Afghan, are known to be at least 2,000 years old, and pictures of dogs that seem to have special attributes have been found on Assyrian rock carvings. The Romans developed some hunting breeds and used dogs extensively as pets.

When did the specialized breeding of dogs begin?

Mankind learned how to breed animals for special purposes very early in history. Other domestic animals such as cows and horses were bred to produce certain results, and men must have applied these techniques to the dog in the early days of civilization.

Breeding was originally controlled in order to produce dogs that could do certain kinds of work, and hunting dogs were among the first to be developed. Since early man depended on hunting for his food, he needed dogs that could chase swift-running animals, bring them to bay and kill them if necessary. Another basic breed was the shepherd dog. When the early tribes settled down to an agricultural life and raised herds of domestic animals, specialized dogs were required to help round up the cattle and sheep. These dogs had to be strong and agile enough to protect a flock against preying animals. A breed that had superior intelligence was necessary, for in handling a flock of animals, there is a great amount of decision-making. Quite often shepherd dogs must use their own judgment.

What were the early dog breeds?

In the Arctic regions the Eskimos and other northern tribes developed several varieties of dogs to pull their sleds. Here specialization was extremely important. A sled dog not only had to be strong enough to pull a heavy load, but it had to have a thick fur coat as a protection against Arctic winters.

Finally, there were pure sporting dogs. All through history men have raced anything that could move, and dog racing can be traced back to the ancient Romans. The greyhound has an ancestry almost as old as any breed and was undoubtedly used in competition thousands of years ago. The Romans also bred dogs for fighting, a cruel sport that fortunately has almost died out in our time.

The American Kennel Club lists over 125 breeds of dogs in existence today. Of course, many breeds are variations of a basic type, but specialized breeding is still going on. Dog breeding has become an involved occupation

How many different breeds are there today?

with many persons trying to produce dogs with unique features. They are bred for a certain size, shape, stance, color, temperament and intelligence. However, the dog family continues to develop on its own, though not scientifically. Random crossbreeding has led to a vast number of mongrels, some of which can be quite interesting.

The variations seem endless, and yet one basic factor remains unchanged. The dog — no matter what it looks like now — is the same animal that owes its heritage to *Tomarctus,* and through *Tomarctus* back to *Miacis,* the animal that began it all 40 million years ago.

The Dog as an Animal

Because of selective breeding the dog has been made into one of the most diversified species on earth. Yet, with all the careful control, the dog has changed only superficially. Every dog belongs to the same zoological family, and even the wild dogs, such as the wolf, are members. The final test is the ability of any kind of dog to produce young with any other kind of dog.

Actually all dogs are really tame wolves, or all wolves are really wild

While wild dogs howl, domesticated dogs bark. In the loneliness of the night, however, a domestic dog may sometimes revert to the habits of its wild ancestors.

SIGHT HOUNDS

SALUKI

BORZOI

OTTER HOUND

AFGHAN HOUND

GREYHOUND

NORWEGIAN ELKHOUND

HARRIER

BEAGLE

BASENJI

HOUNDS

DEERHOUND

SCENT HOUNDS

BLOODHOUND

WOLFHOUND

BASSET HOUND

FOXHOUND

COONHOUND

dogs. Call them what you will — they belong to the family that the zoologists call the *Canidae*.

Canidae is the name that refers to the entire species of dogs and is merely a more learned way of saying canines. The dogs, as chief members of this family, are also members of two other groups. One is the *Mammalia*, or mammals. As a mammal the dog fits all of the requirements. It is a warm-blooded animal, covered with hair or fur, bears live offspring and nourishes its young with milk from its mammary glands.

What names are applied to the dog?

Dogs also belong to the *Carnivora*. Carnivores are meat-eaters with teeth especially developed for cutting, tearing and grinding. All carnivores have clawed feet, powerful bodies and legs adapted for running down game.

There is yet another name that applies only to the dog — the domestic dog. It is *Canis Familiaris*.

Creatures like the giraffe, the hippopotamus and the elephant have one physical feature that is much more developed than the rest of their bodies. Such special features are designed to help them in the task of getting food. In contrast, a dog is a compactly built animal with all of its body components in proportion to each other. This conformity of parts allows the dog to function in all kinds of terrain and conditions. Scientists call the dog a nonspecialized animal that is able to eat many different kinds of food

What are the dog's physical features?

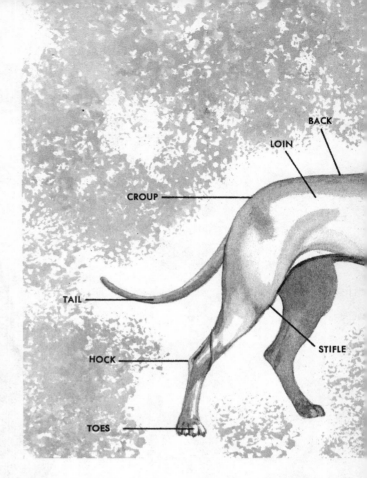

and able to withstand great variations in temperature. This makes for a high-survival type.

Throughout the history of the earth, specialized animals have become extinct because of changes in their environment. These are changes in the conditions that animals need in order to live. This does not seem likely to happen to *Canis Familiaris*. In its ability to survive under many varied conditions, the dog is second only to man, whose complete adaptability makes him the best survival type so far.

A dog has legs and feet adapted for running, and its deep chest is designed to accommodate the great amounts of air needed in a long chase. A straight but fairly flexible back, powerful rear haunches and an erectly set head enable the dog to function as a fighter as well as a runner.

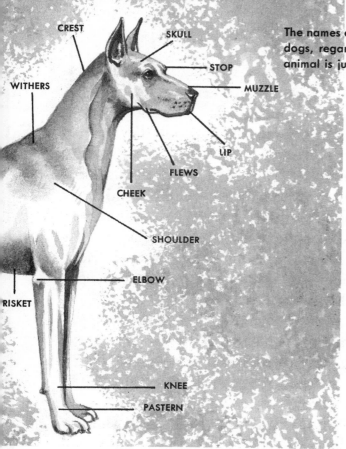

CREST

SKULL

STOP

WITHERS

MUZZLE

LIP

FLEWS

CHEEK

SHOULDER

ELBOW

RISKET

KNEE

PASTERN

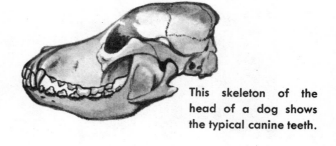

The names of the body parts are common to all dogs, regardless of breed. In dog shows, the animal is judged by excellence of its features.

This skeleton of the head of a dog shows the typical canine teeth.

a dog's mouth a fearful weapon as well as a grinding mill to chew bones.

Secondly, the dog's stomach is supplied with digestive juices that are much stronger than the juices found in many other mammals. These acids readily dissolve the calcium in the bones and allow the dog to eat foods that would make some other animals sick.

There are many variations in the type of hair or fur that covers the dog's skin. Actually, the type of coat that a dog has is determined by climate, its breed and the function of that breed. Dogs from warm countries usually have short, sleek coats, while dogs from colder areas have heavy coats. The northern sled dogs have two coats, as a soft down grows beneath the long, stiff outer fur. Most dogs adapted for work in water have an oily fur that keeps their skin dry when they swim.

There are two basic reasons for the ability of a dog to eat bones.

Why can a dog eat bones? In the first place, the dog has a well developed set of teeth that are built for tearing, cutting and grinding. This allows it to cope with all kinds of food. A powerful set of jaw muscles makes

Some of the dog's senses are superior to those of many other

What kind of senses does a dog have? animals. Its sense of smell, particularly, is almost without comparison. Some breeds, especially those in the hunting and tracking classes, have an extremely acute sense of smell. The bloodhound, often used by police for tracking, can follow a trail that is invisible to other dogs. One sniff of a person's clothing or shoes is enough. The bloodhound can then often track that person for miles across streets, fields and mountains.

An excellent sense of smell is one reason why wolves can silently follow their prey through the forest on the darkest night, unerringly sensing every twist and turn of the trail.

A dog's hearing is also superior. Not only is the dog sensitive to very faint

The first thing you should provide for your puppy is a good bed. There is no need to buy something expensive, as a box with an old cushion or one lined with old blankets will do. It is a useful idea to place a clock under the puppy's sleeping blanket for the first few nights. The ticking sound will make the puppy feel less lonely and help to train the pet to stay in bed.

Housebreaking the puppy is an important part of its education. Feed your pet at regular intervals and take it outside after each meal. If you live in the country, let the puppy run about outdoors as soon as it wakes up in the morning and before it goes to bed at night. If you live in an apartment, or if you are unable to take your puppy outdoors, teach it to use a box filled with torn newspapers. Put the puppy into the box after it has eaten and make your pet stay there until it has done what is expected of it. Change the newspapers every day, but always leave a few soiled papers. Your puppy "remembers" with its nose.

If the puppy misbehaves in the house, punish it only if you catch it in the act; otherwise, the puppy might not know why it is being punished. Spank it with a folded newspaper, and say clearly, "No! No! No!" Then put the puppy out of the house or in its box.

sounds, but it can detect a range of sounds well beyond the perception of a human being. Our hearing covers a range between 50 and 15,000 cycles per second. Above that, most people hear nothing. A dog, however, can hear many thousands of cycles beyond that. There are special dog whistles that produce a sound much too high for man to hear, but within range for dogs. Most dogs can also move their ears to locate the source of a sound.

It is in the sense of sight that the dog becomes a very ordinary animal. Dogs have only average eyesight and some have poor eyesight. Their vision is liable to grow worse with age and the eyes then often succumb to disease. But the dog has a great advantage in the placement of its eyes. They are placed so that the animal can look straight ahead with both eyes. This is known as binocular vision, which is lacking in many animals that have eyes set in the sides of their heads. Such a placement gives the dog a good sense of depth perception. That is why a dog can accurately gauge the distance of objects and jump over obstacles with confidence. Incidentally, recent research is leading some scientists to believe that dogs are color blind and see everything in shades of gray.

Dogs cannot actually talk, but they can

How does a dog "talk"? communicate. They are able to make a wide range of sounds — whines, yelps, growls, snarls, whimpers, barks and howls. These sounds all mean something to a dog, and if it has an understanding master, the dog can communicate many things. It is possible for the animal to show emotions all the way from love to hate by the sounds it makes and to indicate its desires quite clearly.

More important is the fact that a dog can understand its master. Not many species of animals can be trained to understand human speech, but some dogs have been able to respond to more than 150 different words! This is a powerful reason for the close association of man and dog, for communication is a key to all relationships. When living beings can understand each other, friendship is often easily won.

The life span of a dog is between ten and fifteen years, but

How long does a dog live? this is only an average figure. There are several instances of dogs living to twenty years, but these dogs are exceptions to the rule. Experts say that, generally

speaking, a relaxed breed will outlive a nervous breed. Actually, the life span of a dog depends on its heredity, and the nutrition, care and handling it is given from puppyhood on.

Many people reckon each year of a dog's life to be equal to seven years in the life of a man.

Not all dogs are friendly, and strange

Why are dogs so friendly to humans? dogs should be approached with caution, but the species in general is very friendly to man. There are several rea-

Teaching your dog to walk on a leash does not have to be a tiresome job. In the same hand in which you hold the leash, hold a piece of dog biscuit. When your puppy smells the biscuit and sees that you have something good to eat, it will follow along without getting the leash tangled up about your legs. After a few minutes, give the dog the cooky. Soon the dog will learn how you want it to walk on the leash.

It is not too difficult to teach your dog to sit on command. Call the dog to you, slip the leash over its head, and say, "Sit!" Repeat the word, hold the dog's head up with the leash, and press down on its rump. Reward the dog by giving it a bit of food as soon as it is in a sitting position, and pat it to show that you think it is a good dog. Make the dog remain sitting until you say "Up." The more often you repeat these words, the less time it will take the dog to understand what it is you want it to do.

Dogs learn easily and like to work.

help train their cubs in the techniques needed for survival, and they will fight to the death to protect the litter. All this shows a special social instinct equaled only by monkeys, apes and man.

Perhaps the single greatest trait the dog shows is intelligence. This intelligence is evident in almost every breed and shows especially in the wild breeds. As a matter of fact, with the exception of man, the *Canidae* as a whole are among the most intelligent of all the mammals. Dogs can solve problems, remember events, act on their own will and obey orders. This high intelligence has most certainly led the dog as a species to associate closely with man. It was quick to adapt to such a relationship, and in return gave its loyalty and special abilities to the service of man.

How does a dog's intelligence serve man and itself?

No other animal has accompanied and worked for the human race so willingly. No other animal will choose to fight at a man's side rather than seek its own freedom. No other animal will give of its affection so freely.

With their highly developed brains and clever hands, men are far superior to dogs. We know our history and plan for the future; the dog lives only its own life. We can produce wonders of science and works of art; the dog is only an instinctive creature imprisoned within his animal nature.

Yet despite these differences the miracle persists. A man can love a dog and admit it to his life; the dog can accept this love and give its life to the man.

sons for this trait. As noted earlier, the ability to communicate in some fashion with man and the greater ability to understand some of man's speech are strong factors leading to friendliness.

Even in its wild state the dog is a social animal. It seems to like company. Wolves live and hunt in packs and show a great deal of cooperation in chasing their prey. They will take turns in chasing the hunted beast until it is exhausted and then, if it turns out to be a dangerous animal, the wolves will fight it in relays. Most other carnivores live a solitary life and hunt only for themselves. Wolves will often bring food to those that cannot hunt, and a father wolf not only guards its young but also brings food to the lair. Adult wolves

The Specialized Groups

Throughout the history of man's association with the dog we find a slow but steady development of breeds for special purposes. This finally led to the setting up of classifications for types of dogs. All dogs that performed related jobs ended up in a basic group. But more interesting is that most dogs within a group are more closely related to each other in appearance, physical conformation and temperament than to dogs in another group. Yet this does not mean that a dog bred for a particular kind of work cannot do anything else. It just means that it is better adapted for a specific task and will be trained more easily for it. But no matter what a dog is bred for, it can still make a pet and a companion.

There are six main groups, or classifications, of dogs recognized in the world today.

What are the main groups of dogs?

These are the sporting dogs, hounds, working dogs, terriers, toy dogs and nonsporting dogs. To round out the picture a classification should be included that is not officially recognized, since the dogs in the group have no special job, no special appearance, no way at all to standardize a breed. These are the mongrels, the result of accidental breeding.

SPORTING DOGS

Sporting dogs have been carefully bred for centuries and are extremely specialized.

What are the sporting dogs?

They are fairly high-strung, but very willing and friendly animals. Hundreds of years ago, these dogs were invaluable in helping to increase the food supply through their great hunting ability. Today they are

The pointer hunts by running back and forth quickly across a hunting field. When the dog smells a bird, it "freezes," pointing its nose in the bird's direction.

The setter "sits" on its haunches when it finds a bird.

The springer spaniel makes the birds fly into the air.

used mainly by sportsmen who value the skills of such an animal.

Sporting dogs are divided into four subgroups, each with a special skill related to hunting: pointers, setters, spaniels and retrievers. (See pages 8-9.)

How do pointers and setters hunt birds? Pointers and setters are bird dogs — dogs trained to hunt birds. Their development was intensified with the invention of firearms and the beginning of the sport of shooting birds in flight. This hunting technique arose early in the eighteenth century, and as rifles and shotguns were perfected, the various breeds of pointers and setters were improved to meet the very special needs of the hunters.

A pointer or a setter must find game where it lies hidden in the brush. To do this the dog must have an extremely keen sense of smell and must know how to approach the game without disturbing it. This discovery of game is often accomplished well out of sight of the hunter, and a good bird dog will stand motionless, from short minutes to long hours, until the hunter arrives to flush the bird into the air.

The dog must also be sufficiently trained not to move or flinch when the shot passes over its head, and it must wait until ordered to find and return the killed game. This specialized job requires extensive training, beginning in puppyhood. Breeders have gone through many generations developing bird dogs that have the proper nose and proper temperament, and a well-bred pointer or setter makes a fine field dog as well as an affectionate pet.

Where and how did pointers and setters develop? The original stock of pointers and setters came from the area now known as Spain some time in the period between A.D. 500 and 1000.

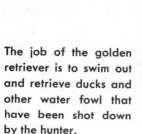

The job of the golden retriever is to swim out and retrieve ducks and other water fowl that have been shot down by the hunter.

Even in those days special breeding was taking place, and the pointers and setters were developed in the British Isles from this Spanish stock. The early varieties of these dogs were used for hunting long before the invention of firearms in Europe.

Pointers were originally used to find game for the chase. They would locate rabbits or deer, indicate the position to the hunters, and then greyhounds or other swift-running dogs were used to bring down the game after it was flushed. The pointers' job did not change too much when firearms began to be used instead of running dogs. Today the pointers still find game in the same manner, but the hunter now shoots instead of releasing another type of dog.

The setter's job has not changed too much either. It became known as a setter because it was supposed to "set" game for the net. Netting birds and small game was a great sport before guns were used. When a setter located the prey, the dog would freeze in position, and the hunter would toss a net over the hidden covey of birds.

Both basic breeds, pointers and setters, have been developed into many varieties, but all are admirably suited as field dogs.

The spaniel, a smaller field dog, was also developed from **Where did the spaniel come from?** Spanish stock, hence its name. Because of its resemblance to the setter family, it is thought that the spaniel may have been one of the original sires

21

of the setter group. When the spaniel was brought to the British Isles, many other breeds were bred into the line, producing a variety of these small, intelligent and friendly dogs.

Like pointers and setters, spaniels operate with hunters in search of small game and birds. They work very closely with their masters and are always in sight. The spaniel does not point or set the game. It runs just ahead of the gunner and flushes game into the open. After the shot, a well-trained spaniel sits motionless until directed to retrieve the game.

How does a spaniel hunt game?

Some spaniels are bred to work in water. These water spaniels retrieve birds that have fallen in streams and lakes, carefully swimming with the game and depositing it at the feet of their masters.

The springer spaniel, a larger and more rough-coated dog, is a different kind of specialist. It works together with a hunter and another dog belonging to the retriever group. This rugged animal flushes or "springs" the game. After the hunter shoots, the retriever is released to return the bird.

The retriever is an example of an entirely "created" breed. No one is certain of the exact origin, but research indicates that at first retrievers may have been bred by crossing spaniels with various hunting hounds, and possibly with poodles to obtain the long curly coat. The result is a large, sturdily built animal,

How were retrievers developed?

equipped to swim in the roughest and coldest water. Retrievers are very friendly dogs and make fine house pets if one does not mind the long fur on the furniture during the shedding season.

Unlike the other hunters in the sporting group, a retriever does not find or flush game. Its only job is to return game to the hunter. Retrievers are used mainly for duck

How are retrievers used in hunting?

The most highly developed sense of smell of any dog belongs to the bloodhounds. For this reason they are widely used to assist police in tracking down escaped prisoners.

hunting (shooting ducks flying over water). They wait patiently with the hunter in a duck blind or other cover until commanded to swim out.

One of the outstanding features found in retrievers is the "soft mouth." The dog is able to grip a bird, wounded or dead, in its large mouth and swim back to the shooting point without leaving a single tooth mark on the game.

Retrievers are also used in sea rescue work because of their great swimming ability. They have large paws and powerful legs, and their long coat is slightly oily to protect the skin against soaking.

HOUNDS

Hound dogs are generally more intelligent and calmer in temperament than sporting dogs, perhaps because they are not so highly specialized. Hounds are solidly-built

Why were hounds bred?

animals that are adapted to running and tracking. They were bred for the sport of running deer, fox, rabbit and other fleet animals. Followed by hunters on horseback, hounds will chase, trap and hold an animal at bay until the men arrive.

The hounds are classified into two broad subgroups, the sight hounds and the scent hounds. (See pages 12-13.)

Sight hounds are mainly runners and jumpers of fantastic speed and agility. In earlier days, sight hounds were used to chase game along broad open stretches. In addition to speed, they had to be able to vault over streams, hedges and walls, and have the strength and fighting ability to kill the game after it was run down.

How are sight hounds used?

Compared with other dogs, their sense of smell is not highly developed. As its name implies, the sight hound must first see its prey and then give chase with the game in sight. Sight hounds are rarely used for hunting today, and they have become mainly pets instead of hunters.

Sight hounds are, historically, the oldest group of dogs in existence. Primitive man did not have the weapons that could kill a bird on the wing or fell a fleeing deer. His dogs had to trap the animal until he could arrive to kill it, and the high-speed running dog was perhaps the first specialized dog bred by man.

What are the oldest known dog breeds?

Of the hounds, the saluki is the oldest known breed. Ancient Egyptian paintings depict the saluki used in the chase, and Assyrian and Sumerian rock carvings show dogs that resemble the modern saluki in every detail. These carvings date back to 6000 B.C.

Both the Afghan and the greyhound also date back to early Egyptian times, when they were used for chasing game over the long, open, barren stretches of the Middle East. The Romans used the greyhound as a competitive racing dog, a function it still performs today.

Sight hounds, obviously bred to be runners, have long graceful legs, slim bodies and pointed noses. Some of the fastest runners have the rear hip joints set at a sharp angle, allowing the rear

The greyhound's tremendous speed makes it suitable for dog races. The dogs chase an electrically-controlled artificial rabbit around a circular track. The first dog over the finish line wins the race.

legs greater flexibility for speeding across uneven terrain. A variation is found in the low-slung dachshund, or badger dog. It originated in France or Germany and was used in Central Europe to hunt small game. The smooth-coated dachshund is a fierce fighter, yet it makes an affectionate pet.

An example of how specialized cross-

What breeds produced the Russian wolfhound?

breeding was once used to create a type is shown in the development of the borzoi, or Russian wolfhound. In the seventeenth century, Russian noblemen imported some salukis, but the severe winters made the dogs extremely uncomfortable. A wise breeder crossed a saluki with a collie, and by the next century he had produced a new type — a slightly heavier saluki covered with a collie's warm fur.

From Ireland comes the Irish wolf-

How big is the largest dog?

hound, the largest of all dogs. Standing on its hind legs, it reaches a height of over six feet, which is taller than the average man. This rugged animal is shaped basically like a shaggy greyhound, and it possesses a powerful jaw. It was bred to chase wolves and the huge Irish elk, though today this purpose has been largely outlived. The Irish wolfhound is an extremely gentle hound. It makes a fine guard dog and devoted companion for children. The only problem in keeping this large animal is the immense amount of food it requires every day.

Scent hounds are dogs that track game

What are scent hounds?

by following a ground scent. It is because of these animals that we can appreciate the special ability that most dogs have — an extremely fine sense of smell. The scent hounds stand at the top of the list in this talent, and they can track game through the roughest terrain.

The bloodhound, which has an average weight of ninety-five pounds, best demonstrates this kind of work. This highly intelligent animal can follow a trail that may be days old. The dog will track it for miles. One police case history in the United States lists a record trek of 138 miles for a bloodhound!

Though widely used by police today, they were originally used by farmers to track stolen animals. The African hunting dog, the basenji, can pick up a scent that is over eighty yards away.

Scent hounds are an ancient group of dogs that must have

How old are scent hounds as a group?

been developed quite early in the history of man. The basenji was used thousands of years ago by the Egyptian Pharaohs, the beagle goes back to the days of the Roman Empire, the basset to early England, the harrier to ancient Greece and the Norwegian elkhound to the period of 5000 B.C. In those early times, the discovery that a dog could follow a trail by scent alone widened the scope of hunting possibilities, as game could be followed through dense forests and overgrown fields. But even more important, speed was not necessary. The cries raised by hunters as they dashed after their sight hounds were also no longer needed. A scent hound following a trail slowly and steadily would eventually lead its master to the game. Hunting could take place on foot and valuable horses would not have to be risked in a chase.

There are many specialized talents among the scent hounds. The bea-

What are some of the special skills of scent hounds?

gle and the basset are used for rabbit hunting. Like the foxhound, they run in packs and show an admirable team spirit as they cut off and surround the game. In the United States, the coonhound is trained to chase and tree its prey. It lets out an extraordinary howl as it runs, which tells the hunter when the dog has found the scent. Another howl, differently pitched, indicates that the quarry has been treed.

The African basenji works quietly, for it cannot bark. Its only sound is a sorrowful yodel, but it is able to drive small game into a waiting net. This dog has recently become very popular as a pet in the United States, for it is an alert and playful animal.

The otter hound is a fine swimmer that has webbed feet. It is trained to dive into the water and catch otter. The use of the otter hound for this purpose, however, is seldom practiced today.

Today hunting is a sport and is no longer needed to increase the food supply. Many hunting breeds are being used as pets.

The Eskimo dog is the "work horse" of the snow-covered lands in the Far North.

WORKING DOGS

Of all the classifications of dogs, the work dogs render the greatest service to man. In general, they are the most intelligent of all dogs. Many of their functions are accomplished without any supervision at all. They make their own decisions and solve problems completely on their own. Work dogs are divided into the following subgroups: sled dogs, sheep dogs, guard dogs and a miscellaneous unit. (See pages 44-45.)

In the Arctic, sled dogs have been in the service of man for over 5,000 years. Although many other breeds have been used as draft animals, only the sled dogs work in teams, pulling loaded sleds over long distances in

How are sled dogs protected against the icy weather?

extremely cold climate. All of the sled breeds closely resemble each other in every way. Their body structure is stocky, with heavy bones and a deep chest. Short powerful legs, broad snow-shoe-type paws and husky haunches give the sled dogs the ability to use their immense strength efficiently.

All the dogs have a long, thick outer fur coat with a soft oily down next to the skin. Their ears are small and somewhat rounded to avoid frostbite. The ears are also furred on the inside as well as on the outer surface. These animals have so much natural protection against the icy Arctic weather that they normally sleep in the snow at temperatures of 50 degrees below zero! A favorite device of the sled dog is to dig a hole in the snow and curl up completely with its bushy tail wrapped around its nose to keep warm.

27

There are not too many variations in the sled dog group, since the weather conditions permit only an animal that is completely adapted to the Arctic. They all seem to have developed from one primitive type of northern dog, and the changes throughout history have not been too great. The Eskimo husky, widely used in Alaska, is perhaps the best known sled dog. Its brother across the Bering Strait is the Siberian husky, which has a longer and taller build. Other relatives are the Samoyed, the spitz, the Norwegian elkhound and the Chinese chow.

What are the different sled dog breeds?

Another relative, perhaps the finest sled dog bred, is the Alaskan Malemute. Named after the Malemiuts, an Alaskan Eskimo tribe which developed the dog, the Malemute is the largest and strongest of all the sled dogs. It was bred from a cross between the Eskimo husky and the wild Arctic wolf. This combination produced a dog with the large-boned, stocky frame of the husky and the flexible back, rangy build and tremendous endurance of the wolf. A Malemute looks more like a wolf than a domestic dog. Its strength, fighting ability and natural intelligence almost always results in its selection as sled team leader. A lead dog disciplines the other dogs, sets the pace, checks the trail for danger and sets a working example to the entire team. Many times a Malemute has led a sled to safety, while its driver was sick or unconscious on the sled.

What dog was crossed with a wolf?

Sled dogs take to their work quite naturally, but the training must begin in puppyhood. In Eskimo tribes this job is given at first to the children, who rapidly become experts in handling puppies. Within a year or two, the young dogs are ready to take their places with the adult animals. A sled team is an economic necessity for the Eskimos, because it is their only form of transportation and their only means of hauling food back to the settlements.

Why are sled dogs important to the Eskimos?

A fully trained team usually contains eight to twelve dogs. In the forested section of Alaska the team works in a line, one behind the other, but the Eskimos of the open Arctic hitch the dogs in a broad fan, each one with its own trace. This spreads the weight of the team over a larger area, a necessary device in this zone of treacherous ice.

Not too many sled dogs have become

How are sled dogs used today?

pets because the breed has not been as widely popularized as other dogs. In addition, an inaccurate idea exists as to their temperament. Most people believe that sled dogs are vicious. This is not so. They are fierce fighters and will not hesitate to take up a challenge from another dog, but they are quite gentle with people. The U.S. Army K-9 Corps was unable to use the sled breeds as patrol dogs because these animals could not be trained to attack a man without provocation.

Today, teams are used for sport in several winter resorts. Vacationers enjoy rides behind a snappy team, and sled racing is another sport widely practiced in many northern areas. In parts of Canada and in northern sections of the United States, sled teams still fulfill their ancient function by delivering mail and groceries when the winter snows close the roads.

Without the sled dog, Alaska would not have been easily settled, and the exploration of the Arctic and the Antarctic would have been delayed for many years. Even today the sled dog is considered essential for certain types of Polar expeditions.

The sheep dogs, or shepherd dogs as

How are sheep dogs helpful to ranchers?

they are more commonly known, are found in every part of the world where people farm and keep herds of domestic animals. The job these dogs perform

Collies (left), and the German shepherd (above), are trusted helpers that are often used to watch over flocks of sheep which might otherwise stray.

goes back to a time before cities were built, a time when the human race became familiar with agriculture and learned how to breed domestic animals for use as food. The ability of the dog to understand the many problems that arise in herding cattle and sheep from one pasture to another, the necessity to drive these animals to another farm or market place, the need to protect them from preying animals — all these reasons made the shepherd dog a valuable asset to early farmers.

But the job has not changed since then. Dogs are still used in the very same manner today. Ranches in the United States, Argentina, Australia and elsewhere still employ shepherd dogs to assist men in the task of raising domestic animals.

There are several types of shepherd dogs. They do not resemble each other physically, but they do share one basic trait — a high degree of intelligence.

Shepherd dogs vary in size and temperament. The **What are the breeds of shepherd dogs?** family of collies and the German shepherd are perhaps the best known, because they have been widely used as pets. Other breeds include the Belgian sheep dog, the Shetland sheep dog, the English sheep dog, the Hungarian puli, the French briard, the Welsh corgi and the Rottweiler, a German descendant of Roman camp dogs. This by no means completes the list, though, because farmers in many countries have adapted other types of dogs for shepherd work. The Norwegians, for example, use the elkhound as a farm animal.

Depending on their size, shepherd dogs **How do the shepherd dogs work?** have different methods of handling a herd of animals. The larger dogs can control a herd by circling, barking and even throwing their weight against the animals. The Shetland sheep dog will run right over the backs of a tightly packed flock of sheep in order to get to the other side and turn the entire group in another direction.

The small Welsh corgi, a cattle herder, handles animals many times its size by nipping at their heels and somehow avoiding the flying hoofs. The corgi has tremendous courage. Many a man has lost heart at the prospect of going into a running herd of frightened cattle, but a corgi will fearlessly dash right into the midst of the mass and control its movements.

A well-trained shepherd dog can handle many animals, make them go where it wants, round up strays and deliver an entire herd to an exact point. Sheepmen especially value their dogs, which are indispensable in controlling a flock.

A shepherd dog lives and works out of **How do the coats of shepherd dogs vary?** doors, and the quality of the coat it has depends on several factors. Many of the dogs that have been bred in the damp climate of parts of the British Isles have a long fur coat to keep their bodies warm. Some of the European shepherd dogs do not need this protection and have a coat of shorter, smoother hair. Dogs that work in thorny or brambly areas need protection in the form of earflaps that hang

During the war, Doberman pinschers (left), worked as sentries, scouts and first-aid assistants in branches of the armed forces.

BOXER

After a long period of training, a seeing-eye dog becomes capable of directing its master with great intelligence.

down to cover the tender inner lining of the ears.

As with any group of dogs that need special qualities, the shepherd dogs have been bred carefully, not only for the job they perform, but also for the conditions of climate and terrain.

Guard dogs are used in almost every kind of police and military work, and they performed important duties while accompanying patrols during World War II. Farmers find them useful for the protection of their animals, and many people living in lonely areas keep guard dogs to assure them of safety. Almost any dog can be trained for guard work, but throughout the years

What are the qualities of guard dogs?

special breeds have emerged as best fit for the job. A guard dog should be big, agile and willing to fight. It must be completely obedient and loyal to its master or trainer.

31

Two breeds of dogs have been used extensively as guard dogs. One is the German shepherd and the other is the Doberman pinscher. Both were developed in Germany, a country that seems to have specialized in this function for dogs. From Germany also comes the great Dane and the boxer. These dogs, along with the Doberman, were specially bred from other dogs that had some of the desired fighting characteristics. The boxer was bred from an early mastiff, and the Doberman owes its size to an early smooth-coated shepherd and the rottweiler. The boxer's temperament and courage come

What breeds were developed as guard dogs?

from the black and tan terrier. The English developed the mastiff and the bull mastiff to the ranks of guard dogs, and both breeds have often been used as the basis for developing other kinds of guard dogs.

All of these animals are big-boned and have heavy, powerful jaws. They have a reputation for being vicious, but anyone who has owned a great Dane or a boxer can vouch for its gentleness with children.

Rescue work of various kinds has brought about the development of some miscellaneous canine types. The Newfoundlands were bred as ship's dogs to work with sea-rescue teams. The big, brawny animal is built to swim in heavy seas. It can take a drowning man in tow and bring him safely to shore.

What dog can save a drowning person?

The Saint Bernard is a gentle household pet. It was formerly used to find lost travelers in the Alps.

Even today, in the century of the automobile, the Bouvier des Flandres is still used as a cart dog in the Low Countries of Europe, particularly in the rural districts of Belgium and Holland.

In the European Alps the Saint Bernard performed a unique service. Named after the monastery of Saint Bernard in Switzerland, where the breed was developed by monks about 1,000 years ago, these dogs were trained to find travelers lost in the heavy snows of the mountains. The animal's sense of smell led it unerringly to the lost traveler, even if the man were buried under the snow. Then it barked loudly as a signal to the rescue team. Around its neck, the dog carried a container of food and medicine. The Saint Bernard is little used for this purpose today, as foot travel in the Alps is now far less frequent than it used to be.

What dog was developed by Swiss monks?

Some dogs are cattle drovers, helping men drive cattle along the roads from the farm to the market. In this group are the German schnauzer and the Belgian Bouvier des Flandres. These huge dogs have also been used to pull small carts in many rural sections of Europe. They are cheaper to maintain than cart horses. Farmers also find them useful for general herding and guarding.

Dogs have guided blind people for centuries, but only in the twentieth century has there been a proper system devised for the training of such animals. A guide dog, or seeing-eye dog as it is often called, must be intelligent, calm-tempered and large enough to physically influence its master's movements. It should come as no surprise that the best guide dogs come from the shepherd group. After all, leading a blind person is in itself a form of shepherd work. The German shepherd dog and the collie seem to be best suited for guide work, although the boxer has also been used successfully.

What dogs are best suited as guides for blind persons?

The training of a guide dog is rigorous and is started when the dog is very young. But just as important as training the dog, is training the blind person who is to be guided, for dog and man must work as a team.

TERRIERS

The terrier group contains one of the largest selections of breeds to be found in any class. There are many varieties of these scrappy, bright and alert little dogs. Every type of coat exists in the terrier group from short, smooth hair to rough, curly fur. Almost all are small dogs, often with more courage and daring than the larger breeds. For their size the terriers are strong animals and fast runners. (See pages 36-37.)

The name *terrier* is derived from the Latin *terra,* meaning

Why are they called terriers?

"earth." It is actually almost a description of the job that terriers perform — that of hunting small animals on the ground and even in their burrows. In other words, a terrier is a dog that goes to the earth to hunt.

It is an extremely difficult hunting assignment. To chase a groundhog, fox, or weasel into its hole and then fight and kill the animal takes great courage. A terrier actually fights an animal on that animal's own terms and in its own territory. No other dog faces so great a challenge.

Almost all terriers were developed in the British Isles. In

Where are the terriers from?

some cases the origin is unknown, but many seem to have been bred from larger dogs, possibly hounds and mastiffs of different kinds. What the terrier breeders were seeking was a short-legged dog with a flexible back and a coat that could withstand rough underbrush. Today's terriers show that the breeders succeeded in their task, and they also succeeded in developing dogs that were friendly and loyal to people.

Terriers are among the most popular of pets. Because they are small, they take well to living in apartment houses. They eat moderate amounts of food and

It is important to pick up a puppy correctly.

RIGHT   WRONG   WRONG

enjoy the company of children. They are liable to be a bit high-strung, but this characteristic only makes them more playful.

TOY DOGS

There are fifteen breeds in the class known as toy dogs — all are tiny and alert. From the point of view of temperament, these miniature dogs can be among the most aggressive, a quality for which there is good reason. (See pages 40-41.)

Throughout their history, toy dogs have had two functions — to be pets and ratters.

For what purposes were the toy dogs originally used?

They were used during the Middle Ages to chase rats that infested the dark halls of castles, and it is for this job that they needed to be fierce little fighters. But they were also bred to be pets, perhaps the only group originally so designed.

Court ladies liked to be able to carry a pet dog in their arms or on their laps, and these little furry animals were suited for the purpose. They were used as ornaments to a lady's costume. Sometimes they served another function. In the Middle Ages sanitary conditions were almost nonexistent, and dogs were allowed to rest on their mistresses' laps to attract fleas. It was a strange job and one which, fortunately, is no longer necessary.

Today the toys are exclusively pets. They make good companions for people who want a dog, but do not have the room for a larger breed.

A collar with a little purse attached, containing the owner's name, his address, and some money to make a telephone call, is an aid that often results in retrieving a lost dog.

My name is HAPPY
I belong to
Margot Wolf
Tel.: JU 7-9014

There are special food dishes for breeds of long-eared dogs.

Special carrying cases for puppies and small breeds are used when the animals are transported in public means of transportation.

It seems fairly certain that all the toy dogs were bred down in size from larger dogs,

How were the toy breeds developed?

although the origin of many is now completely lost. The Pekingese, once the sacred dog of China, has been known for over eight centuries. It is sometimes called the "lion dog" because of its appearance, or the "sleeve dog" because Chinese

TERRIERS

AIREDALE

CAIRN TERRIER

WELSH TERRIER

KERRY BLUE TERRIER

SCHNAUZER

IRISH TERRIER

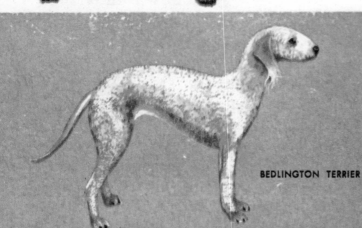

BEDLINGTON TERRIER

SEALYHAM
TERRIER

DANDIE DINMONT
TERRIER

SCOTTISH TERRIER
(CLOSE-UP OF HEAD)

SCOTTISH TERRIER

WEST HIGHLAND WHITE

BULL TERRIER

MANCHESTER
TERRIER

SKYE TERRIER

nobles used to carry it in the wide sleeves of their robes.

The Pomeranian was bred down from spitz stock in Germany, while the Spanish papillon is really a tiny spaniel. The famous Mexican Chihuahua is thought to have descended from the techichi, a sacred dog of the Mexican Toltecs, but the Mexican hairless dog is believed to be of Asiatic origin.

The toy poodle was bred for people who liked large poodles, but who wanted a version more suitable for smaller quarters.

NONSPORTING DOGS

Nonsporting dogs, bred originally for special purposes, are primarily kept as pets today. They are related to other dogs but have achieved an appearance and function that is unique.

The list of nonsporting dogs is a small but distinguished one. **What dog is able to get along well with horses?** The Dalmatian, a spotted dog resembling the pointer, is the famous coach dog of history. It was employed to follow the horse-drawn carriages and served as a guard dog for the occupants when they traveled through bandit-infested territory. The Dalmatian lopes along effortlessly mile after mile, never tiring, always alert. It gets along well with horses, and many of the early horse-drawn fire companies in the United States kept Dalmatians as pets.

The poodle, another well-known nonsporting dog, has an ancient ancestry. **What dog is one of the most popular of pets?** This curly-coated dog has served as a shepherd, a water retriever and watchdog. It is one of the most intelligent of dogs and is used frequently in circus performances. Poodles of all sizes have become some of the most popular pets in the world. They are so popular that beauty salons for poodles exist in some large cities where the dogs are specially groomed and clipped.

China has given us the chow, the only dog with a blue tongue. **What dog has a blue tongue?** The chows are related to the sled dogs through the Samoyed, which was bred with a Tibetan mastiff to produce the breed. The chow was used for many purposes in ancient China — as a guard dog, hunter, retriever and court companion.

Bulldogs and the Boston terrier also belong to the nonsporting class of dogs.

MONGRELS

Mongrels, the result of accidental cross-breeding represent an unofficial class of dogs. They exist in every size, shape and color. Most are quite intelligent because of the lack of inbreeding, which sometimes reduces intellect in closely-bred dogs. Since mongrels rarely breed true to any type, each generation of these dogs poses a guessing game.

DALMATIANS

NONSPORTING DOGS

POODLE

CHOW

BULLDOG

BOSTON TERRIER

JAPANESE TOY SPANIEL

ENGLISH TOY SPANIEL

POMERANIAN

YORKSHIRE TERRIER

MANCHESTER
TOY TERRIER

TOY DOGS

GRIFFON

MALTESE TERRIER

MEXICAN
HAIRLESS

WHITE TOY POODLE

ITALIAN GREYHOUND

BLACK TOY POODLE

PEKINGESE

AFFENPINSCHER

MEXICAN CHIHUAHUA

PAPILLON

MINIATURE
PINSCHER

PUG DOG

Mongrels usually become pets and

Do mongrels have any use?

many a grown man can fondly remember a mongrel dog he had as a child. One does not have to spend a large sum of money for such a dog, and sometimes these animals can be acquired free of charge. Careful selection and the ability to recognize some of the parent breeds will result in the acquisition of a fine, useful dog.

Mongrels have been used for almost every type of job that a purebred dog has done. This has happened because most mongrels have a strong strain of specialization in their backgrounds, a trait that serves them well when men require their services.

They have also done well as performing circus dogs. Many show business dog acts contain a high percentage of mongrels, and trainers in this field look carefully for desired traits. Some of the dog acts that can be seen on television are staffed with intelligent and hardworking mongrels, perhaps the only class of dogs in the world that exists to entertain and amuse the public.

 # Shows and Trials

Men are a competitive race and it was inevitable that they would soon begin to compare their dogs to determine the best performers. Such tests must have begun early in history, and today, dog shows and field trials are serious events with keen competition.

Basically, a dog show is held to determine the best dog in

What is the value of a dog show?

each breed. With the cooperation of kennel clubs all over the world, sets of standards have been drawn for each breed. In the shows, dogs are checked and tested to see how well they conform with an idealized standard.

Dogs that win in shows are highly valued as breeders and very often earn large sums of money for their owners. The puppies of a champion dog are eagerly purchased by people who may want to use the dog for its specific function, or by those who merely want a pet that rates high in its class.

It has often been said that the judging at a dog show results in the selection of dogs that conform to high standards of appearance, but that cannot do the working job of the breed. However, years of experience have shown that dogs that are consistent winners will do just as well in practical field trials as other dogs.

Actually, people who are serious about the breeding and training of dogs respect the dog shows, because they assure the proper continuance of each type.

A large dog show will contain several judging rings, and several breeds are examined at the same time. Before the dogs are brought into the rings they must be set on a bench for public viewing. When a specific breed is ready to be judged, the dogs are taken to the proper ring by the owner or a handler. There they are inspected by a judge who is attended by a steward and a dog club official.

How is judging at a dog show done?

All the dogs are then walked around the ring so that the judge can see if they have the proper gait for the species. Then they are all faced in the same direction, and the judge inspects each one individually. He checks the stance, body conformation, color, teeth, eyes, feet and bone structure. He will often examine the body of a dog with his hands, feeling for the proper placement of legs, shoulders and hips. He will sometimes test the strength of some animals by pressing down on their rear haunches. Some judges will even face two terriers, nose to nose, and wait for them to bristle. A timid terrier is not representative of its breed.

Finally, the dogs are walked one at a time — toward and away from the judge — so that he can check their movement in terms of their function. Then he makes his decision, taking into consideration all the points to be judged, including the attitude and temperament of the dog.

What are the various awards in dog shows?

The winning dog must now compete against the previous champions, which have not been part of this preliminary test. This time the winner is

A prize at a dog show is a coveted award for every owner of a show dog. Even the dog seems proud.

WORKING DOGS

CHOW

KUVASZ

SIBERIAN HUSKY

NEWFOUNDLAND

AUSTRALIAN KELPIE

SAMOYED

ALASKAN MALEMUTE

BERNESE MOUNTAIN DOG

SPITZ

KOMONDOR

GREAT DANE

BOXER

GREAT PYRENEES

WELSH CORGI

ROTTWEILER

PULI

BELGIAN
SHEEP DOG

OLD ENGLISH
SHEEP DOG

There are special contests for working dogs. Here a police dog is shown during achievement exercises.

Winners of dog shows are always unusually fine animals. They set a standard for all other dogs, a standard that is followed by dog breeders everywhere. They also have another effect. Consistent winners sometimes cause fads among people who keep dogs as pets. The popularity of such pets depends on which breed is currently in favor.

Why are field trials held?

Field trials serve as the area in which the actual working functions of each breed are tested. They are very important for men who want to use their dogs as more than just pets. Here appearance is not so important as function. The dog must perform its job efficiently in order to win.

When shepherd dogs are tested, actual herding situations are set up. The dogs are timed and judged very carefully as they work. They must solve problems deliberately created for them, and sometimes unexpected ones as well. One such incident occurred at Madison Square Garden in New York City, during a demonstration of sheep herding. A flock of sheep was let into the arena, and a work collie was brought in to round them up and drive them into a pen. But the sheep became excited by their surroundings and broke in several different directions. Many raced up the aisles among the spectators, but the hard-working collie painstakingly ran up and down the steps sorting out the sheep from the people. The dog finally collected all the sheep and drove them into the pen.

Hunting dogs are also the subject of intensive field trials, where they are

declared *Best of Breed*. Since every dog belongs to a basic group, all the Best of Breed are gathered into their respective groups and a similar competition takes place to determine the *Best of Group*. In the final event, the group winners compete for the *Best in Show*. A dog judged Best in Show represents its own breed better than any other dog of another type. Actually, this honor is not as important as Best of Breed, which serious dog handlers prize above all others, for it means they have a dog that will earn money for them as a breeder.

checked for tracking, pointing, retrieving and steadiness under gun fire. It is in the field trials that the true mettle of a dog is tested.

Dogs learn very easily to respond to the wishes of their masters, and this trait is tested in obedience trials. Dogs must walk properly with their owners on or off the leash. They must come to heel when commanded, sit when ordered and remain in position no matter how far away their owner walks, and no matter how long he waits. They must learn to be quiet and calm in the company of other dogs and to perform complicated maneuvers.

What are obedience trials?

One of the interesting things about obedience training is that an owner must take a course at the same time as his dog. Both learn together the principles of cooperation. It helps to make a dog a more social animal, a better and more controllable pet and an obedient assistant when working.

The dog was the first wild animal to be domesticated by man, and this intelligent animal has long been known throughout much of the world as "man's best friend."

The Wild Dogs

WOLF

Although man has thoroughly domesticated the dog and even changed its appearance, habits and temperament, there are still untamed wild dogs roaming the relatively undeveloped areas of the world. They run free, preying on other animals, and live the same kind of life they did thousands of years ago.

These dogs have not changed too much since the time primitive man began his domestication of animals. They furnish a strong clue as to the types of dogs that existed when man began breeding them for special purposes.

There are a handful of distinctive types among the wild dogs, but most are variations of the original primitive breeds. The wolves are a completely separate breed. Their differences are slight adaptations to the climate and terrain of the countries in which they live. North America has several kinds of wolves. The two most common varieties are the timber wolf and the Arctic wolf. Wolves still roam the Siberian steppes and parts of Europe, but they will gradually disappear as more and more of the land space on earth is taken up by man's rising population.

What animals are classed as wild dogs?

The coyote is still found in large numbers in the United States. Its main

TIMBER WOLF

ARCTIC WOLF

DHOLE

COYOTE

HYENA

range is the Southwest, but coyotes have also been seen in the Northeast and in parts of Canada. An interesting phenomenon is the result of crossbreeding coyotes and domesticated dogs. The result is known as a coydog, which may be the beginning of a new breed.

Jackals live in Asia, North Africa and in parts of southeastern Europe. They vary in color, depending on the country of origin. These animals run in packs and a large group will very often menace outlying settlements. They prey on domestic animals and have been known to attack men.

The hyena is found in the Near East and in India. It hunts alone, usually at night, and feeds on carrion.

The Asiatic dhole is a large, vicious, red-furred dog. It has been known to hunt down the large Asian buffalo. Dholes range all the way from Siberia down into India. They destroy game and domestic animals, particularly in remote areas.

The wild dog of Australia is the dingo. It originally lived in Asia, but was taken to the island continent by aborigines in their migration tens of thousands of years ago. The dingo is no longer a purebred, having mixed with some of the dogs that European settlers brought with them. These wild dogs are a great problem to sheep ranchers in Australia, who hunt them down **mercilessly.**